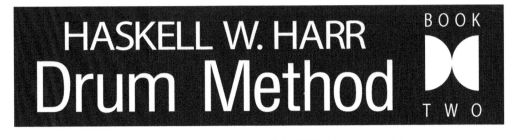

HASKELL W. HARR Drum Method — BOOK TWO

T0039492

FOREWORD

■ Drum rudiments are fundamental rhythmic patterns which will aid in developing basic techniques for drum playing. They **are not** a complete system, or method for teaching drums, but they do supply us with material for hand development and acquaint us with short rhythmic patterns which will be found in drum music.

The 26 rudiments in this book are placed in the order set forth by the N.A.R.D., which uses the first thirteen for their entrance examination. It is not necessary to study them in this order; divide them into four categories according to their importance.

Phase 1. Single stroke roll, single and double paradiddles, plus the single stroke exercises, lessons 6 through 17 in Book 1.
Phase 2. The roll. For additional application use exercises 25 through 29 in Book 1.
Phase 3. The flams, and all exercises using flams.
Phase 4. The ruff, and all rudiments using the ruff.

The pages in this book are numbered in continuation of Book 1. ■

The Author,

Haskell W. Harr

ISBN 978-1-4234-0773-7

HAL•LEONARD® CORPORATION
7777 W. BLUEMOUND RD. P.O. BOX 13819 MILWAUKEE, WI 53213

Visit Hal Leonard Online at
www.halleonard.com

CONTENTS

A Rudiment is the first principle of any art or science. **Drum Rudiments** are the first principles of the art of drumming. Notes are placed in groups to form the rudiments in the same manner as letters are placed in groups to form words.

The explanation and sticking of the twenty-six rudiments in this method are written as adopted by the **National Association of Rudimental Drummers,** a group of Nationally known drummers from all parts of the United States. The rudiments are as follows:

1. The long roll
2. The five stroke roll
3. The seven stroke roll
4. The flam
5. The flam accent
6. The flam paradiddle
7. The flamacue
8. The ruff
9. The single drag
10. The double drag
11. The double paradiddle
12. The single ratamacue
13. The triple ratamacue
14. The single stroke roll
15. The nine stroke roll
16. The ten stroke roll
17. The eleven stroke roll
18. The thirteen stroke roll
19. The fifteen stroke roll
20. The flam tap
21. The single paradiddle
22. The drag paradiddle No. 1
23. The drag paradiddle No. 2
24. The flam paradiddle-diddle
25. The Lesson 25
26. The double ratamacue

EXPLANATION OF BOOK NOTATIONS

Throughout the book, rudiments will be referred to by their numbers as listed above. For example: A circle number two ② placed over a note would indicate a five stroke roll, a circle six ⑥ the flam paradiddle, etc. Numbers placed in a square, ▣ designate measure numbers.

Each exercise has all of the rudiments used therein, with their numbers, placed at its beginning.

CARRYING THE DRUM

To carry a drum on parade, rest the sling on the **RIGHT SHOULDER,** allow it to pass **diagonally across the body,** front and back, and hook together just above the **left hip.** Adjust the sling so that the **TOP HOOP** of the drum is approximately **THREE INCHES BELOW THE WAIST,** just far enough to have a slight bend in the **right elbow** when the stick strikes the center of the drum. The drum should rest directly in **FRONT OF THE LEFT LEG.** A leg rest fastened to the drum will assist in steadying the drum when marching.

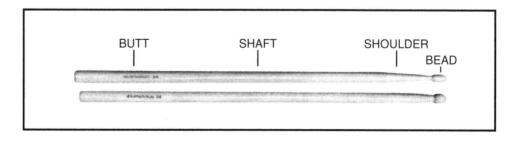

In order to develop TECHNIQUE, CONTROL, and the proper ATTACK and RELEASE, it is necessary for the student to have the correct method of holding his drumsticks. There are many ways of holding drumsticks, depending on the style of drumming being done. The beginner should start with the traditional method, as taught in this book.

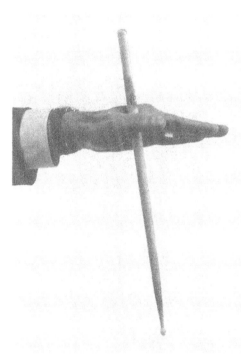

FIGURE 1

THE LEFT HAND

Extend the left arm, palm of the hand down, fingers together, as shown in the picture at the left. Place the stick in the SOCKET between the THUMB and FIRST finger, with one-third of the stick (from the butt end) above the hand. The grip should be just tight enough to cause a slight drag if you try to pull the stick from the hand. Study figure 1.

Close the third and fourth fingers and TURN THE ARM TO THE LEFT. The stick will then fall into position **across** the **third finger,** as shown in figure 2.

Draw the arm towards the body, allow the first and second fingers to CURL TOWARDS THE STICK to act as a guide for the stick, and you will have the closed hand position for playing as shown in figure 3.

Your hand should now be in the following position: Stick BETWEEN thumb and first finger, FIRST TWO FINGERS lightly against the stick, THIRD FINGER CLOSED and acting as a **support** for the stick, FOURTH FINGER resting against the third. **The thumb is always above the stick.**

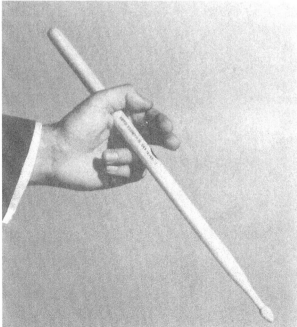

FIGURE 2

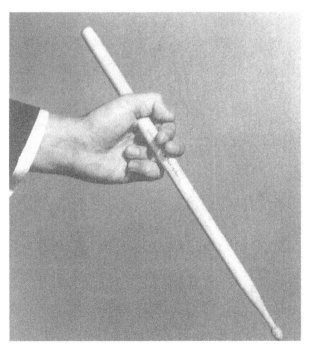

FIGURE 3

HOLDING THE RIGHT STICK

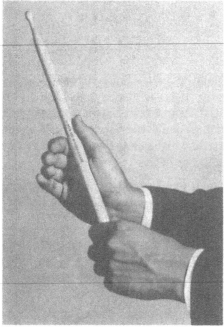

FIGURE 1

Place the stick DIAGONALLY across the PALM of the hand. Grip between the FIRST FINGER and the THUMB one third of the distance from the butt end of the stick. Figure 1.

Close the fingers LOOSELY around the stick. The SECOND FINGER will be used to **help control the stick.** Figure 2.

TURN THE HAND OVER, so that the BACK of the hand will be up when playing. The stick will be approximately in a straight line with the wrist and arm. Figure 3.

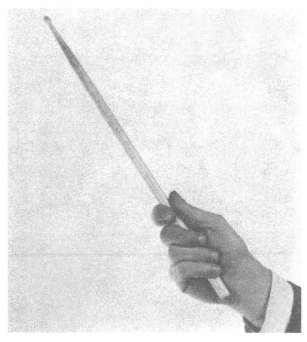

FIGURE 2

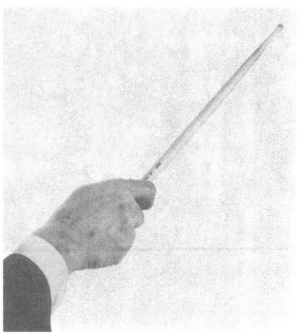

FIGURE 3

POSITION: Stand erect (all practicing should be done while standing), have the drum in a position so that the head will be about five inches below the waist.

THE RIGHT STICK

Place the bead of the stick on the head, slightly off center. Raise the arm until the hand is on a level with the chin, at the same time turn the wrist outward, causing the bead to travel in a half-circle. See dotted line in figure 1.

TO COMPLETE THE STROKE, return the stick to the head with a motion similar to **cracking a whip.**

Be sure that the drum is low enough to allow the arm to hang nearly straight down.

Practice the following exercise until each of the notes can be struck evenly with the same amount of force. See that they are spaced evenly. Take your time, be sure that the stroke is made correctly.

R — Right stick

FIGURE 1

R R R R R R R R R R R R R R R R R R R R R R

THE LEFT STICK

Place the bead of the stick on the head. Raise the arm until the hand is on a level with the chin, at the same time turning the wrist outward. To complete the stroke return the stick to the head with a motion similar to **flipping water from the fingers.**

Be sure that the wrist is turned out as the arm is raised. Many make the mistake of raising the arm straight up and down without turning the wrist. The stick must be free.

Another common error is to hold the stick tightly across the third finger knuckles with the thumb. To avoid this, have the thumb touch the first joint of the first finger.

Practice this exercise the same as the one above.

L — Left stick

FIGURE 2

L L L L L L L L L L L L L L L L L L L L L L

ALTERNATIVE THE STICKS

OFF CENTER
CONCERT DRUM

CENTER
PARADE DRUM

In the previous lesson we studied how to play with each stick individually. We will now start to use both hands, one after the other, called ALTERNATING.

Draw a circle on the head, or pad, about two inches in diameter, in the CENTER OF THE DRUM. The object of the circle is to keep the sticks as close together as possible when playing.

The pitch of the drumhead varies. The tone in the center of the head is dead, due to the strain applied by the tension rods pulling from all sides. The farther away from the center you play the higher the pitch of the tone.

If you would play with one stick near the center of the drum and the other stick about half way between the center and the hoop, you would have two different pitches and the playing would sound uneven.

By playing with each stick an equal distance from the center of the head you will have an even tone. Study the diagram at the left.

Check the sticks to see that they are of the same weight. This may be done by striking them on a hard surface. If they are the same, the pitch of each stick will sound the same when struck.

Study the exercise below, pay particular attention to the sticking, notice that at first you have four beats with each hand, then three, then two and then one. Use the same amount of force for each blow, space the notes evenly. Count out loud.

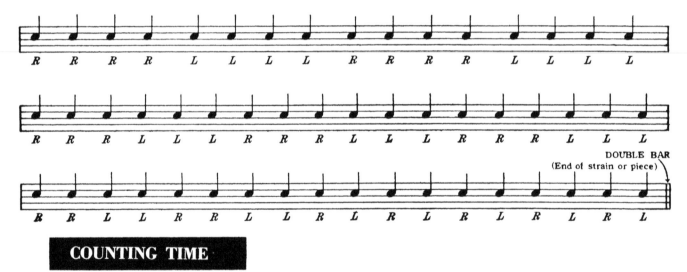

COUNTING TIME

It is very important to have a method of "COUNTING TIME" to develop and maintain a **perfect sense of rhythm.**

A good musician DOES NOT use a VISIBLE means to BEAT TIME, but to the beginner any mechanical means that will aid in gaining musical expresson, especially in counting time is advisable. Of the different methods used, I believe the use of the foot and the voice to be the best for the drummer.

In using the foot to beat time, raise it from the floor slightly, then lower it and raise it again. Thus ↓ down ↑ up. When the foot touches the floor the beat starts. To complete the beat the foot must raise and come down again.

The use of the voice allows even greater division of notes than the foot. In a measure of 4/4 time count 1-2-3-4, one beat for each quarter ncte. To divide the quarter note into eighth notes and count them, add the word "and" after each number, thus: 1 and (&) 2 & 3 & 4 &. The quarter notes may be divided into sixteenth notes and easily counted by adding the letter "E" after the 1, and the syllable "Ah" after the AND, thus 1 e & ah, 2 e & ah, 3 e & ah, 4 e & ah

ROLLS

The drum, being an instrument of percussion, gives forth a short, snappy tone for each note that is struck, regardless of the length of the note, or the amount of force used in the attack.

All other instruments of the band and orchestra are enabled to sustain each note for its designated length, by either drawing a bow across the strings, or blowing air through the tubing. Therefore, it will be necessary for the student to study a method of sustaining the longer notes.

This method of sustaining the notes is done with a series of short notes, played by alternating the hands in rapid succession, called rolls. As each stick strikes the drumhead, it rebounds. This rebound must be controlled, so as to have as much force as the stroke itself, otherwise the roll will be uneven.

Much time and patience will be required to develop a good smooth roll. It must be started slow and gradually increased in speed, for evenness in drumming is the most important factor. Once that a drum-mer has developed a smooth roll, he will not change the speed to fit the tempo of the music. Instead, he will either add or subtract the number of strokes to, or from, his roll according to the tempo. For exam-ple: a half note in a slow tempo would require many more strokes than a half note in a fast tempo.

A drum-beat loses its identity after sixteenth notes, therefore we may use the thirty-second note as a basis for the roll, at a march tempo. Example: two eighth notes tied together, 𝅘𝅥𝅘𝅥 with two lines drawn through the stem of the first, designate a roll. The number of thirty-second notes contained in the first note of a roll, plus the one tap of the note to which it is tied, gives the name to the roll.

All rolls in this method will be analyzed down to the thirty-second notes.

THE CONTROLLED REBOUND of the LEFT STICK. Make the stroke with the same snap used in playing the single strokes. Immediately after the stick contacts the head, apply pressure with the thumb by roll-ing it slightly to the right, thereby forcing the stick back to the head for the second blow. At the same time turn the wrist outward, allowing the third finger to pick up the stick as before.

Left Hand Study.

THE CONTROLLED REBOUND of the RIGHT STICK. Immediately after the stick has rebounded from the first blow, apply pressure towards the bead of the stick by bearing down lightly with the knuckle of the index finger, forcing the stick back to the head. When the stick hits the head the second time tighten the grip with the second finger and snap the wrist outward as before.

Right Hand Study.

As soon as the student has mastered the rebound, he should start alternating the hands, using single strokes at first to enable him to have smooth arm and wrist movement, then bounce each stick to form the Long Roll.

R   R   L   L   etc

2. THE FIVE STROKE ROLL

The Five Stroke Roll is played from "Hand to hand." It starts and stops with the same hand, a second roll will start with the opposite hand from the hand that finishes the first roll. The Five has three primary hand movements RLR or LRL, the first two are bounced, the last stroke is always a single stroke. It may have an accent at the beginning or one at the end depending on whether the roll starts on the beat or finishes on the beat. Practice both ways.

Analysis:

Play the following exercise with single strokes, then repeat and bound the sticks on each sixteenth note. Notes in the ties will develop into the five stroke roll.

3. THE SEVEN STROKE ROLL

The SEVEN STROKE ROLL is not played from hand to hand, it usually starts with the left hand and ends with the right hand. This roll is designated two ways, first by the quarter note (♩) and second, by the same notation as a five stroke, except that a seven is written above the notes (♫). Practice this roll with an accent on the first tap for use when it starts on the beat, and with an accent on the last stroke when it ends on the beat.

Start with the right stick if the roll **starts on the beat,** with the left stick if it **ends on the beat.**

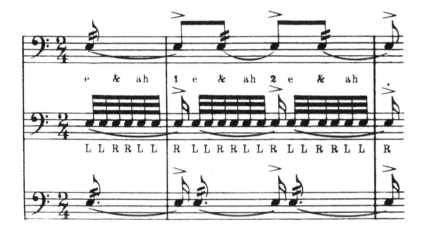

As notated in most rudimental drum solos.

Rudimental interpretation — start on the "e" of the count.

All seven stroke rolls in this book should be played in this manner.

The modern notation of the seven stroke roll.

4. THE FLAM

The Flam plays such an important part in drumming, that it is well to thoroughly understand it before attempting to play it. It is a combination of a stroke and a tap. The difference between the stroke and tap is as follows: A stroke is made with an arm and wrist movement, while the tap is made with the wrist alone. It is written by placing a small note (grace note) before a large note (♪♩). Beats containing Flams should not be attempted until the Flam is mastered otherwise the effect will be lost.

The purpose of the Flam is to broaden the sound of the tone. The sticks do NOT strike the head at the same time, but they must strike so close together that it will sound as one stroke.

The Flam gets its name from the hand that plays the principal note. There are three flams, the right flam, left flam, and the alternate flams. Alternate flams are played from hand to hand, the hand that plays the stroke of the first flam stays close to the drum to be in position to play the grace note of the second flam. This develops a swinging motion from side to side. Many students develop the swinging motion and yet strike the same stick first each time, usually the right, instead of reversing the position. Avoid this error.

Study the starting positions carefully. Start slow; speed will take care of itself.

THE RIGHT FLAM

Hold the right stick at chin level, stick pointing up. Make a right stroke and just before the stick hits the head, drop the left stick onto the head, saying "FA" as the left stick hits the head, "LAM" when the right stick contacts the head. As the control improves, the FA-LAM will close to FLAM, the way the beat should sound. When practicing stop both sticks about 2 to 4 inches above the head.

THE DOWN STROKE

Start with the stick high, make a stroke, then stop the stick 2 to 4 inches above the head, depending upon the beat which follows the downstroke.

Practice the exercise below for the development of the flam. Keep the right hand high while playing the grace notes. After playing the fourth grace note with the left hand make the stroke with the right hand.

L L L L *R* L L L L *R* L L L L *R* L L L L *R* L *R* L *R* L *R* L *R*

THE LEFT FLAM

Start with the **left** hand high stick pointing up. Hold the bead of the **right** stick about two inches above the drumhead. Make a **left** stroke and just before the stick strikes the head drop the bead of the **right** stick onto the head, saying "FA" as the right stick hits, "LAM" when the left stick hits. As your technique develops the FA-LAM will close to FLAM, which is the way the rudiment should sound.

THE UP STROKE

Start with the bead of the stick two inches above the drumhead. Strike the head by turning the wrist in (elbow should snap out), then raise hand to chin level, stick pointing up.

Study for the development of the LEFT flam.

Keep the left hand high while playing the four taps with the right hand. After the fourth tap make the stroke with the left hand.

R R R R *L* R R R R *L* R R R R *L* R R R R *L* R *L* R *L* R *L* R *L*

ALTERNATE FLAMS. FLAM ACCENTS

ALTERNATING THE FLAMS is very important to the drummer, and will require much practice. Start with the **right** stick high, the bead of the **left** stick two inches above the drumhead. Play the grace note with an **UP STROKE** (see previous page), play the main note with a **DOWN STROKE.** The sticks are now in position to play the next flam. As the control improves and you increase the speed, the main strokes will be played closer and closer to the drum.

When playing flams one hand should always be higher than the other.

NO. 5. FLAM ACCENT NO. 1

The Flam Accent No. 1 is composed of a flam and two taps, usually played with two groups of three notes together ( ). The sticking is quite simple, the stick being alternated, except on the grace note of the flam, which is played with the same hand that plays the stroke before it. It may be counted Flam-2-3-Flam-2-3, or Flam-left-right-flam-right-left.

FLAM ACCENT NO. 2

The Flam Accent No. 2 is also used in 6/8 time. Carefully study the sticking. Notice that the sticks do not alternate. Three taps are made with each hand.

UP STROKE

THE FOUR STROKE RUFF

The Four Stroke Ruff is composed of four notes, three grace notes and the principle note. It is very effective if properly executed. The three small notes are played lightly and the fourth note is accented. It is used extensively in numbers of the patrol nature. It is played with single strokes, generally from left to right, L R L R.

Start with the left stick four inches above the drumhead, the right stick straight up. Play a right flam and stop both sticks four inches above the drumhead. Make a left tap, with an up-stroke, raising the hand high, then two right taps from the four inch level. Hold the right stick down. The sticks are now in position to play the next paradiddle, which is sticked in reverse.

To overcome the difficulty in playing the last two notes of one paradiddle and the grace note of the next all with the same hand, hold one stick four inches from the drumhead, the other stick high. Play the three grace notes with the low, follow immediately with the high stick.

Closing and opening the flam paradiddle. Start very slow, gradually increase the tempo. Space the notes evenly. Do not play the single taps faster or lighter than the other beats.

♩=120 M M

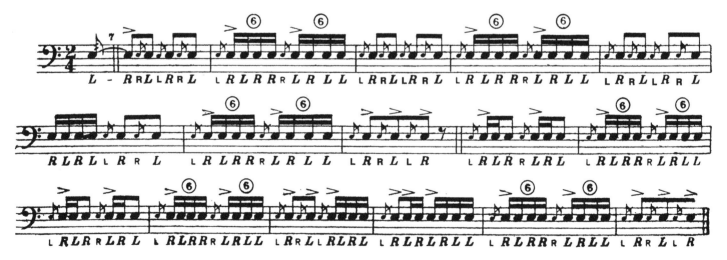

The following exercises are for the application of the ⑥ Flamadiddle. Start slowly and build up the speed to a marching tempo.

78

The FLAMACUE consists of a group of five notes, of which the first and last notes are played as flams. Start the beat with the RIGHT HAND FLAM. Play the second note with a down-stroke of the left hand, with a strong accent. Play the third note with an up-stroke of the right hand and the fourth note with a single tap by the left hand. Your hands are now in position to play another right hand flam for the fifth note. This is one the most used of the rudiments. It may be played from hand to hand, although it is most commonly played by starting with the right flam.

Study for the application of the Flamacue
Exercise No. 1
"Jimmy Mavrik"

No. 3. Seven Stroke Roll
No. 4. The Flam
No. 7. The Flamacue

HARR

No. 2. Five Stroke Roll
No. 3. Seven Stroke Roll
No. 4. Flam
No. 7. Flamacue

Exercise No. 2
"Dan Lynch"

HARR

The following street beats are for the application of the Flams, Rolls of various lengths, Flamadiddles and Flamacues.

Exercise No. 3
"Biddy Oats"

No. 2. Five Stroke Roll   No. 7. The Flamacue
No. 3. Seven Stroke Roll   No. 4. The Flam

Exercise No. 4
"Stanley Satter"

No. 2. Five Stroke Roll   No. 6. Flam Paradiddle
No. 3. Seven Stroke Roll   No. 7. The Flamacue
No. 4. The Flam

Exercise No. 5
"Harold Pitcock"

No. 3. Seven Stroke Roll   No. 6. Flam Paradiddle
No. 4. The Flam   No. 7. The Flamacue

8. THE RUFF

The RUFF is made up of two grace notes and a principal note. It is played with the same motion as the Flam. The two grace notes are played with the low hand. All three notes should be spaced evenly. Start slowly, gradually increase the speed, at the same time apply more pressure to the accented note.

9. THE SINGLE DRAG

The SINGLE DRAG is made of two grace notes and two principal notes. It is a hand to hand rudiment. Play the grace notes with an upstroke of the left hand, the first note with a right right tap, and the second, or accented note, with a left stroke.

The Single Drag is used by many professional drummers to replace the five stroke roll in extremely fast passages.

Start this exercise slowly, watch the sticking carefully. The purpose of the study is to gradually build up the RUFF and the SINGLE DRAG. The numbers in the circle represent the rudiment number.

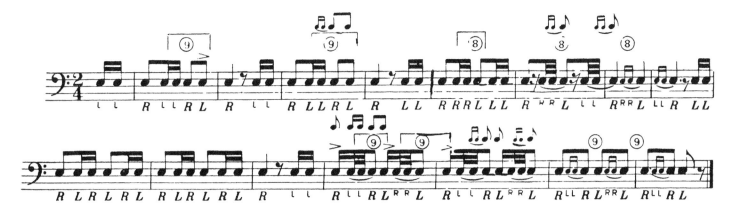

THE GENERAL

Rudiments used: No. 9, Single Drag; No. 3, Seven Stroke Roll; No. 4, The Flam; No. 8, The Ruff.

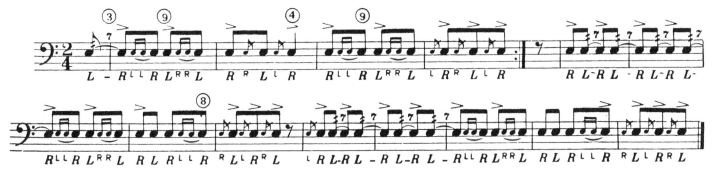

12. THE SINGLE RATAMACUE

The SINGLE RATAMACUE is made up of two grace notes, a triplet and a single accented note. The two grace notes are played with the left hand, the first note with a tap by the right hand, the second note with the upstroke of the left hand, the fourth note with the right hand and the accented note with a stroke of the left hand. The rudiment is played from hand to hand.

Exercise for the application of the ⑫ Single Ratamacue, ④ Flam, ⑥ Flamparadiddle, ⑦ Flamacue, and the ② Five Stroke Roll.

HARR

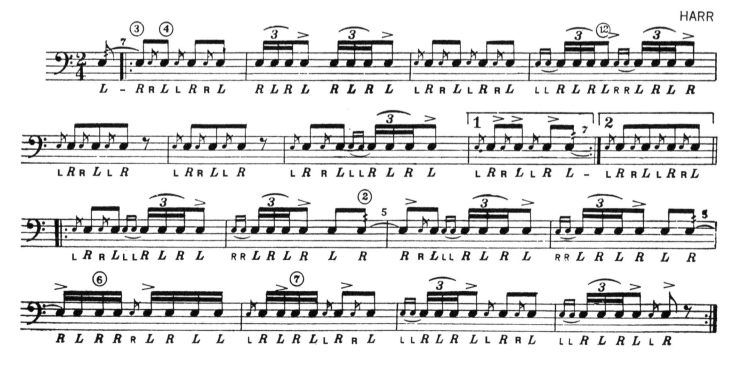

84

13. THE TRIPLE RATAMACUE

The TRIPLE RATAMACUE is made by tripling the first movement of the Single Ratamacue. Play two light lefts, a right tap; two light lefts, a right tap; two light lefts, a right tap, a left tap with an upstroke, a right tap, and an accented beat with the left. The rudiment is played from hand to hand.

Exercise No. 1; For application of the Triple Ratamacue. The rudiments used are as follows:

No. 3. Seven Stroke Roll
No. 4. The Flam
No. 6. The Flam Paradiddle

No. 7. The Flamacue
No. 12. The Single Ratamacue
No. 13. The Triple Ratamacue

Exercise No. 2; The rudiments used are as follows:

No. 4. The Flam
No. 6. The Flam Paradiddle
No. 7. The Flamacue

No. 12. The Single Ratamacue
No. 13. The Triple Ratamacue

14. THE SINGLE STROKE ROLL

The SINGLE STROKE ROLL is one of the most important fundamental beats on the snare drum. A well developed single stroke roll makes a powerful and flashy forte roll. The single stroke rolls are the fundamental beats of all rolls.

Start slowly, with hands raised high. As you increase the speed, the sticks will gradually come closer to the drumhead. When you have attained your greatest speed, gradually start decreasing, at the same time raise the sticks higher accordingly.

R L R L R L R L R LRL RL RL RL etc.

15. THE NINE STROKE ROLL

The NINE STROKE ROLL is played from hand to hand, the same as the five stroke roll. This roll has five primary strokes, the first four are bounced, the fifth stroke is played single. The roll is designated by a quarter note tied to an eighth note (𝄽 ♪). Practice this roll by applying the accent first to the first stroke, then to the last stroke.

Play the following exercise the first time with single strokes. The second time bounce the sticks on all sixteenth notes. The notes in the tie will form the nine stroke roll.

For the application of the Five stroke roll, the Seven stroke roll, and the Nine stroke roll.

16. THE TEN STROKE ROLL

The TEN STROKE ROLL is played by adding a single accented note to the left Nine Stroke Roll. The added stroke is played with the hand opposite to the one which plays the ninth stroke. The rudiment does not reverse.

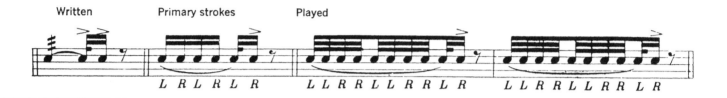

17. THE ELEVEN STROKE ROLL

The ELEVEN STROKE ROLL does not play from hand to hand. It starts with the left hand and ends with the right. The roll is used to advantage in such solos as the "Three Camps", the "Austrian", and the "Hessian", in which the roll is written out. By playing the eleven stroke roll slightly more open, it may be used nicely in 6/8 march tempo where a roll designated by a dotted half note is required. The roll has six primary strokes, three with each hand. The first five are bounced, the last is a single stroke.

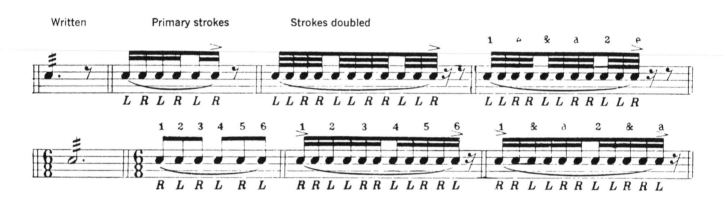

18. THE THIRTEEN STROKE ROLL

The THIRTEEN STROKE ROLL is played from hand to hand. It has seven primary strokes, four with the right hand, three with the left, or reversed. In 2/4 measure, the roll commonly starts on an off-beat and ends with an accent on the beat. The thirteen stroke roll may be used in 6/8 march tempo by playing it more open, to fill in the roll designated by a dotted half note tied to an eighth note.

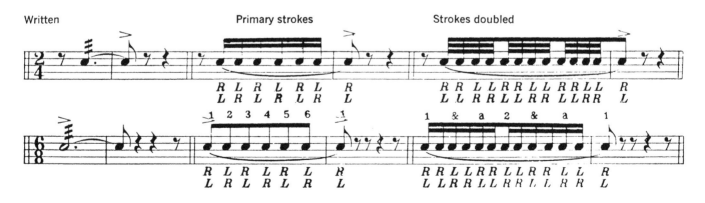

DAWNING OF THE DAY

Count 4 beats per measure.

No. 2. Five Stroke Roll
No. 3. Seven Stroke Roll
No. 9. Single Drag
No. 15. Nine Stroke Roll

BREAKFAST CALL?

Count 4 beats per measure, as if written in **4/8** time.

THE THREE CAMPS

Using 5, 10 and 11 stroke rolls.   DRUM SOLO

The most common interpretation of this solo is to play it as if written in 12/8 time. This will permit all of the rolls to be played in even rhythm. See examples below.

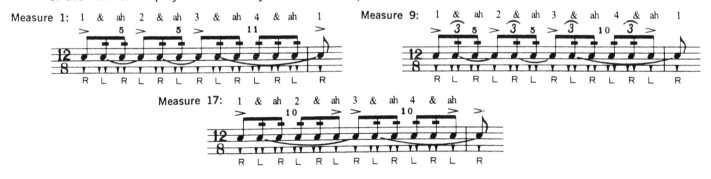

19. THE FIFTEEN STROKE ROLL

The FIFTEEN STROKE ROLL is a one-way roll starting with the left stick and ending with an accented right stick. If starting on the beat, the roll should then start with the right stick.

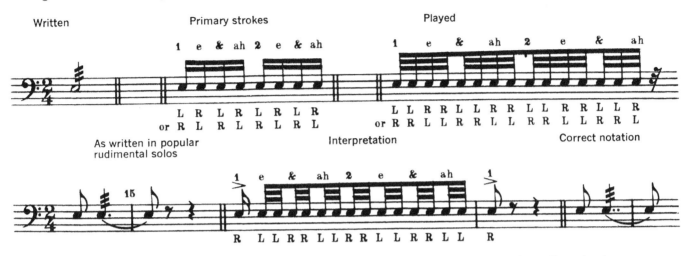

The SEVENTEEN STROKE ROLL, although not listed as one of the twenty-six rudiments, is a very important roll. It is played from hand to hand, although it is never written in series. There are nine primary strokes, five with the right hand, and four with the left hand. The first eight are bounced, the last is a single stroke.

A study for the application of the ② Five, ⑮ Nine, ⑱ Thirteen, and Seventeen stroke rolls.

20. THE FLAM TAP

The FLAM TAP is made up of a flam, followed by a tap. The tap is played with the same hand that plays the principal note of the flam. The Flam Tap is a difficult beat to play at a fast tempo, requiring much practice to master it. The flam tap is used in 2/4 measure and is played from hand to hand. The beat, FLAM ACCENT No. 2, used in 6/8 measure, is often called the FLAM TAP. It is beat the same, but the rhythm is slightly different.

A study in the application of the FLAM TAP. Other rudiments used are as follows:

No. **2.** Five Stroke Roll
No. **3.** Seven Stroke Roll

No. **4.** The Flam
No. **6.** The Flam Paradiddle

No. **7.** The Flamacue
No. **20.** The Flam Tap

"Marvin Richards"

HARR

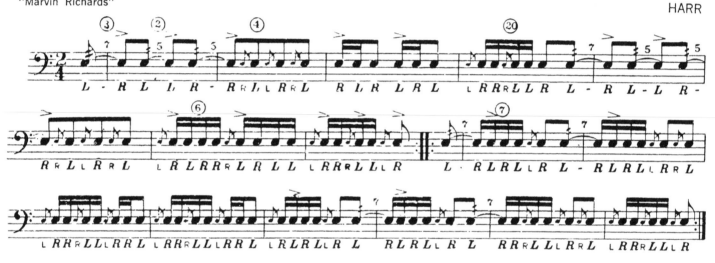

Subjects: No. **3.** Seven Stroke Roll
No. **4.** The Flam
No. **6.** Flam Paradiddle

No. **15.** Nine Stroke Roll
No. **20.** Flam Tap

"Robert Phelan"

HARR

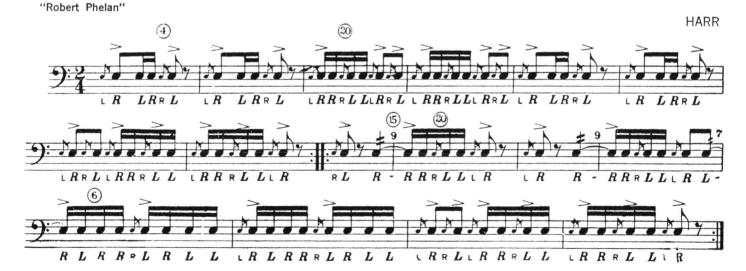

21. THE SINGLE PARADIDDLE

The SINGLE PARADIDDLE is composed of four sixteenth notes. When written in street beats and marches, the paradiddle is generally used in pairs, it being a hand to hand rudiment.

To play the paradiddle, make the first tap with a down-beat to get the accent, the second tap with an upstroke of the opposite hand (the upstroke is executed by playing a tap while the hand is raising) and the third and fourth taps with the hand that played the first tap. Making the second tap with an upstroke, places that hand in a high position ready to play the first accented tap of the following paradiddle.

When practicing, always start slow and gradually increase your speed. Use the word Paradiddle to guide you, saying "PAR-a-did-dle", etc., as you practice. Be sure to space the notes evenly.

Often times the student has difficulty in keeping the last two taps as strong as the previous ones, especially when increasing the tempo. I would suggest that you practice the rudiment with a slightly heavier accent on the last two taps. Example: "par-a-DID-DLE, par-a-DID-DLE."

Exercise for the application of the SINGLE PARADIDDLE. Other rudiments used are:

No. **2.** Five Stroke Roll
No. **4.** The Flam
No. **7.** The Flamacue

No. **21.** The Single Paradiddle
No. **15.** Nine Stroke Roll

STUDIES FOR THE APPLICATION OF THE PREVIOUS RUDIMENTS

Exercise No. 1
"Harlan Morris"

No. **4.** Flam
No. **2.** Five Stroke Roll
No. **3.** Seven Stroke Roll

No. **15.** Nine Stroke Roll
No. **21.** Single Paradiddle
No. **7.** Flamacue

HARR

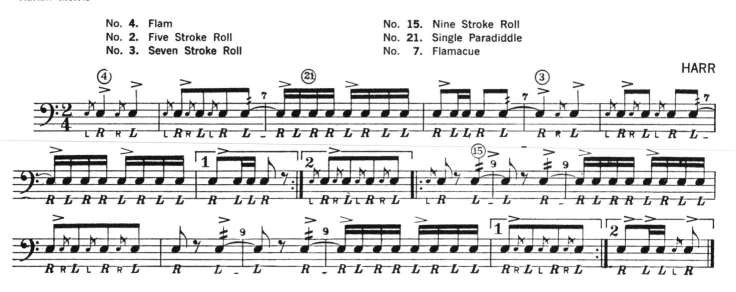

Exercise No. 2
"Floyd Brown"

No. **2.** Five Stroke Roll
No. **4.** The Flam

No. **21.** Single Paradiddle
No. **3.** Seven Stroke Roll

HARR

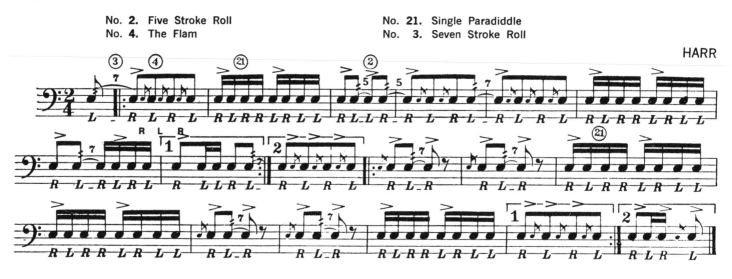

Exercise No. 3
"Richard Lannen"

No. **3.** Seven Stroke Roll
No. **4.** The Flam

No. **15.** Nine Stroke Roll
No. **21.** Single Paradiddle

HARR

94

22. DRAG PARADIDDLE NO. 1

The DRAG PARADIDDLE No. 1 starts with an accented stroke, made with the right hand, followed by two grace notes, played with the left hand, a right tap, a left tap, with the upstroke, and two taps with the right. This puts the left hand in position to start the next drag paradiddle.

A study in **3/4** time.

Study in **6/8** measure introducing the Drag Paradiddle No. **1**, the Flam accent (No. **5**), the Double Drag (No. **10**) and the Double Paradiddle (No. **11**).

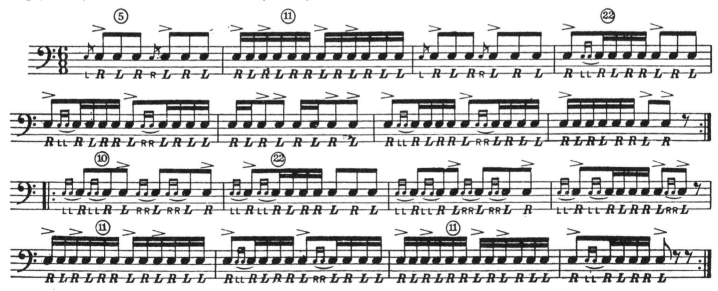

23. DRAG PARADIDDLE NO. 2

Start the DRAG PARADIDDLE No. 2 with a right hand accented stroke, then play two grace notes with the left, a tap with the right, two grace notes with the left, a right tap, a left tap (upstroke) and two right taps. This leaves the left hand raised in position to start the next Drag Paradiddle. The movement is played from hand to hand.

"Hill on the Wabash"

No. **3.** Seven Stroke Roll	No. **6.** Flam Paradiddle
No. **4.** Flams	No. **23.** Drag Paradiddle No. 2

"Billy Marnoff"

No. **3.** Seven Stroke Roll	No. **8.** The Ruff	No. **15.** Nine Stroke Roll
No. **6.** Flam Paradiddle	No. **7.** The Flamacue	No. **23.** Drag Paradiddle
	No. **12.** Single Ratamacue	

HARR

D. C. al 𝄐

24. THE FLAM PARADIDDLE-DIDDLE

The FLAM PARADIDDLE-DIDDLE is played with a right flam, a left tap, two right taps and two left taps. It is played from hand to hand.

25. LESSON TWENTY FIVE

The rudiment, LESSON 25, is played with two light lefts, a tap with the upstroke of the right hand, a left tap, a right accented stroke, two light lefts, a right upstroke, a left tap and an accented right stroke.

Exercise
"George Hall"

No. **4.** Flams
No. **3.** Seven Stroke Roll

No. **7.** Flamacues
No. **25.** Lesson 25
No. **20.** Flam Tap

HARR

26. THE DOUBLE RATAMACUE

Played with two light left taps, a right tap, two light left taps, a right tap, a tap with the upstroke of the left, a right tap and a left accented stroke.

STUDIES FOR THE APPLICATION OF LESSON 25

Other rudiments used are as follows:

No. **2.** Five Stroke Roll
No. **3.** Seven Stroke Roll
No. **4.** Flams
No. **6.** Flam Paradiddle

No. **7.** Flamacue
No. **18.** Thirteen Stroke Roll
No. **20.** Flam Tap
No. **23.** Drag Paradiddle No. 2
No. **25.** Lesson 25

Exercise No. **1**
"Robert Allen"

HARR

Exercise No. **2**
"Raymond Williams"

HARR

COMPOUND STROKES

The COMPOUND STROKES No. 1 and No. 2, are not listed among the 26 drum rudiments, although they are used quite frequently in the fancy street-beats and solos. It will be well worth your time to study them.

COMPOUND STROKE No. 1

COMPOUND STROKE No. 2

Exercise No. 1: Compound Stroke No. 1
"Don Kermeen"

HARR

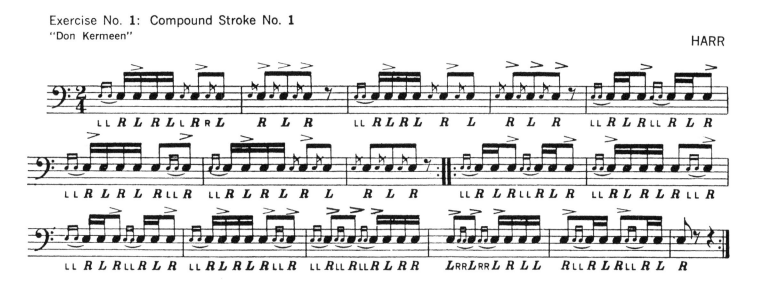

Exercise No. 2: Compound Stroke No. 2
"John Gibson"

HARR

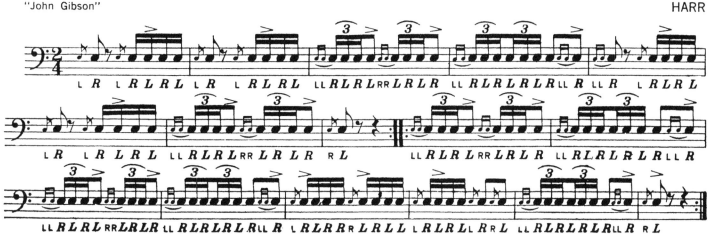

JUDGMENT IN APPLYING THE RUDIMENTS

Very few drum parts are written with the rudiments shown in the manner in which they are taught in the instruction books. Most parts are written with just the single notes, giving the drummer the alternative of playing the parts as written, or of "filling in" by adding flams and ruffs, thereby forming his rudiments. The addition of the flams and ruffs will require considerable good judgment on the part of the drummer, as the application of the wrong accent may destroy the whole rhythm of a number. It may be necessary, at times, to omit an accent.

On the scores below I have written a number of measures of time figures and passages taken from different compositions. On the line below each measure I have shown how the application of flams and ruffs will change the figure to one of the rudiments.

Judgment in Applying the Rudiments (continued)

STUDIES IN 3/4 MEASURE

Start slowly, count three to each measure, gradually increase the tempo.
Rudiments used in the following exercises:

No. **4.** Flams		No. **20.** Flam Tap
No. **7.** Flamacue		No. **22.** Drag Paradiddle No. 1
No. **9.** Single Drag		No. **23.** Drag Paradiddle No. 2
No. **11.** Double Paradiddle		No. **24.** Flam Paradiddle-Diddle
No. **15.** Nine Stroke Roll		

"Mildred Waltz"

HARR

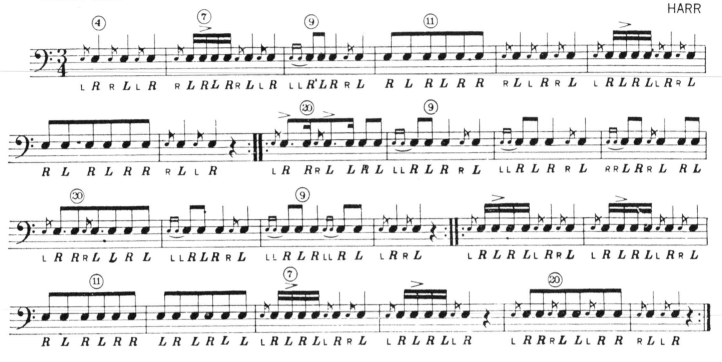

"Julia Waltz"

HARR

Studies in 3/4 Measure (continued)

Rudiments used are as follows:

No. **2.** Five Stroke Roll
No. **3.** Seven Stroke Roll
No. **4.** Flams
No. **15.** Nine Stroke Roll

No. **7.** Flamacues
No. **9.** Single. Drag
No. **18.** Thirteen Stroke Roll
No. **24.** Flam Paradiddle-Diddle

"Covington Waltz"

"Bear Grass Waltz"

Studies in 3/4 Measure (continued)

The rudiments used in this exercise are as follows:

No. **2.** Five Stroke Roll

No. **4.** The Flam

No. **7.** The Flamacue

No. **10.** The Double Drag

No. **18.** Thirteen Stroke Roll

No. **22.** Drag Paradiddle No. 1

No. **24.** Flam Paradiddle-Diddle

No. **25.** Lesson 25

Start slow, count three beats to a measure.

"Agnes Waltz"

HARR

Studies in 3/4 Measure (continued)

Subjects in this exercise are as follows:

No. **2.** Five Stroke Roll	No. **8.** The Ruff	No. **15.** Nine Stroke Roll
No. **3.** Seven Stroke Roll	No. **11.** Double Paradiddle	No. **20.** Flam Tap
No. **4.** The Flam	No. **12.** Single Ratamacue	No. **22.** Drag Paradiddle No. 1
No. **7.** Flamacue	No. **13.** Triple Ratamacue	No. **26.** Double Ratamacue

"Gertrude Waltz"

HARR

Medley 6/8 Rhythms (continued)

STUDIES IN 6/8 MEASURE

Exercise No. **1**

The following exercises are for the application of the rudiments in 6/8 time or measure. Start slowly, counting six beats to the measure. The figures in the circle designate the rudimental number. The rudiments used are as follows:

No. **2.** Five Stroke Roll   No. **7.** The Flamacue   No. **9.** Single Drag
No. **4.** The Flam   No. **10.** The Double Drag   No. **24.** Flam Paradiddle-diddle
     No. **22.** Drag Paradiddle No. 1

The rudiments used in this exercise are as follows:

No. **2.** Five Stroke Roll   No. **7.** The Flamacue   No. **15.** Nine Stroke Roll
No. **3.** Seven Stroke Roll   No. **11.** Double Paradiddle   No. **18.** Thirteen Stroke Roll
No. **4.** The Flam

Exercise No. **2**

108

Studies in 6/8 Measure (continued)

Start all exercises slow, then gradually increase the speed. The rudiments used are as follows:

No. **2.** Five Stroke Roll
No. **4.** The Flam

No. **7.** The Flamacue
No. **11.** Double Paradiddle
No. **12.** Single Ratamacue

No. **9.** Single Drag
No. **26.** The Double Ratamacue

Exercise No. **3**

Study your rudiments carefully. Nine are used in the next exercise.

No. **4.** The Flam
No. **7.** The Flamacue
No. **10.** The Double Drag

No. **11.** Double Paradiddle
No. **12.** Single Ratamacue
No. **13.** Triple Ratamacue

No. **18.** Thirteen Stroke Roll
No. **22.** Drag Paradiddle No. 1

Exercise No. **4**

Studies in 6/8 Measure (continued)

Subjects: No. **3.** Seven Stroke Roll   No. **20.** Flam Tap
    No. **4.** Flams   No. **8.** The Ruff
    No. **5.** Flam Accent   No. **10.** The Double Drag

Exercise No. **5**
"Far-down"

Subjects: No. **2.** Five Stroke Roll   No. **10.** Double Drag
    No. **3.** Seven Stroke Roll   No. **15.** Nine Stroke Roll
    No. **5.** Flam Accent   No. **19.** Fifteen Stroke Roll
    No. **8.** Ruff

Exercise No. **6**
"Dedekii"

D. C. al 𝄌

110

STUDIES IN CUT-TIME ¢

When playing in this tempo, music is played twice as fast as it is written. In other words, a whole note will receive two counts; a half note, one count; etc.

Subjects:

No. **3.** Seven Stroke Roll:

No. **15.** Nine Stroke Roll:

No. **25.** Lesson **25**

This exercise is written in cut-time. Compare the rudiments with the chart shown above. Count: **1** &, **2** &, etc.

Exercise No. **1**

This exercise is the same as No. **1.** When played in tempo, Exercise No. **1** should sound the same as No. **2.**

Exercise No. **2**

Studies in Cut-Time (continued)

"Ned Kendalls"

D. S. al 𝄌

"Robert Simpson"

HARR

Studies in Cut-Time (continued)

"Bob Buggert"

HARR

Studies in Cut-Time (continued)

"Peter Gruber"

SIXTH INFANTRY

No. 2. Five Stroke Roll
No. 3. Seven Stroke Roll
No. 4. Flams
No. 5. Flam Accent

No. 6. Flam Paradiddle
No. 7. Flamacue
No. 15. Nine Stroke Roll
No. 18. Thirteen Stroke Roll

POST'S

No. 3. Seven Stroke Roll
No. 4. Flam
No. 6. Flam Paradiddle
No. 7. Flamacue
No. 9. Single Drag

No. 12. Single Ratamacue
No. 18. Thirteen Stroke Roll
No. 20. Flam Taps
No. 23. Drag Paradiddle No. 2

DIXIE

★   + = Strike the left stick with the right stick, near the shoulder of stick.

PRINCE EDWARD

NEWPORT

No. **2.** Five Stroke Roll
No. **3.** Seven Stroke Roll
No. **4.** Flams
No. **8.** Ruff

Compound Stroke No. 1
Compound Stroke No. 2
No. **25.** Lesson 25

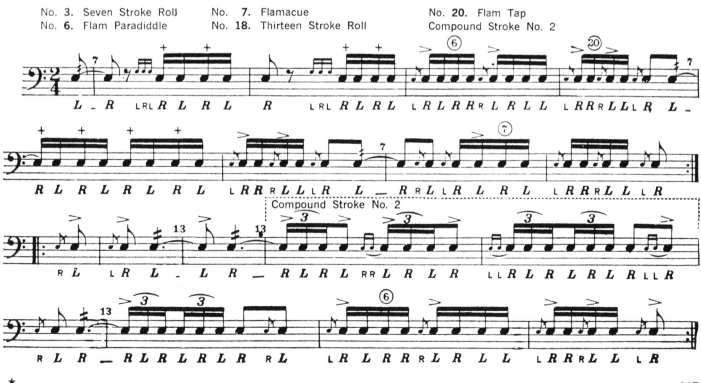

GOVERNOR'S ISLAND

No. **3.** Seven Stroke Roll
No. **6.** Flam Paradiddle

No. **7.** Flamacue
No. **18.** Thirteen Stroke Roll

No. **20.** Flam Tap
Compound Stroke No. 2

★
+ = Stick Beats. Hit right stick with left.

117

DOWNSHIRE

No. **3.** Seven Stroke Roll
No. **4.** Flams
No. **6.** Flam Paradiddle

No. **7.** Flamacue
No. **18.** Thirteen Stroke Roll
No. **23.** Drag Paradiddle No. 2

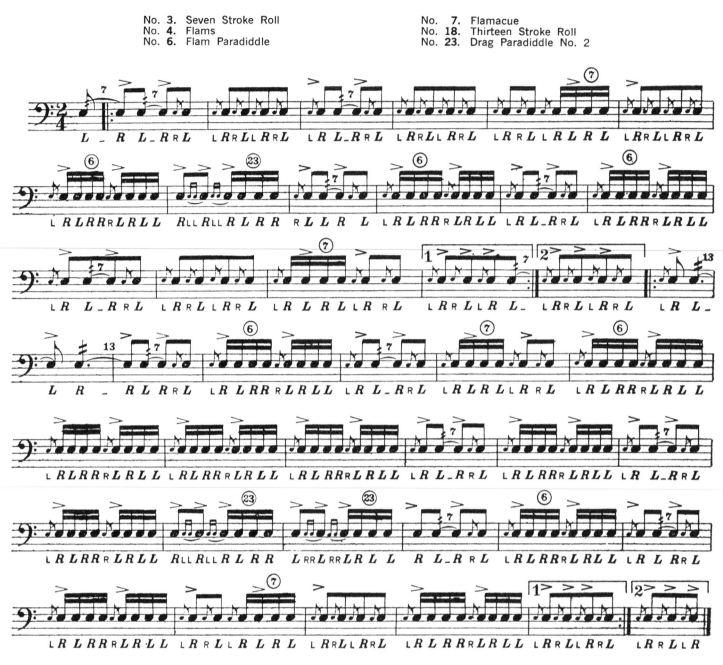

KING WILLIAM

No. **3.** Seven Stroke Roll
No. **4.** Flams

No. **6.** Flam Paradiddle
No. **7.** Flamacue

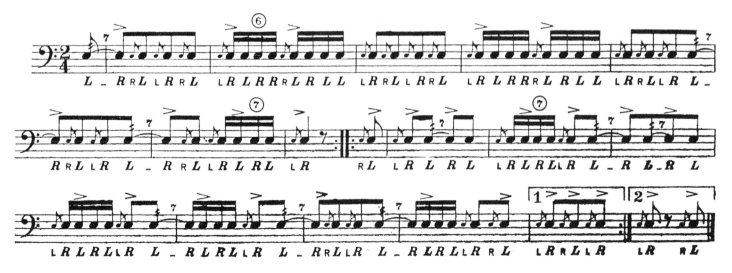

CUCKOO QUICK STEP

No. 3. Seven Stroke Roll   No. 18. Thirteen Stroke Roll   No. 23. Drag Paradiddle No. 2
No. 6. Flam Paradiddle   Full Drag

COL. ANDREWS

No. 2. Five Stroke Roll   No. 6. Flam Paradiddle   No. 20. Flam Tap
No. 3. Seven Stroke Roll   No. 7. Flamacue   No. 25. Lesson 25
No. 9. Single Drag   No. 18. Thirteen Stroke Roll No. 23. Drag Paradiddle No. 2

CAPT. WHITINGS

ANCIENT AND HONORABLE ARTILLERY

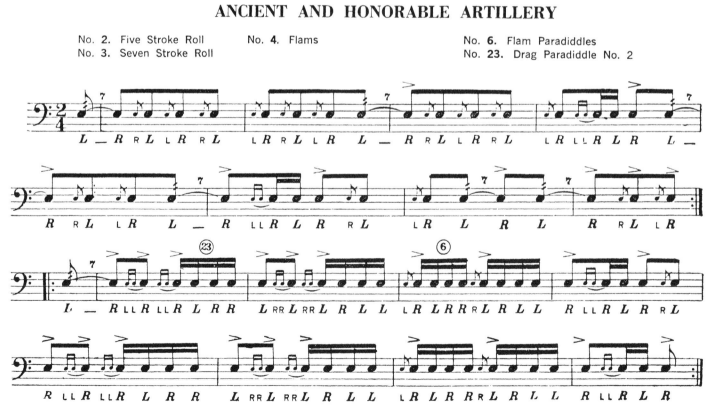

THE GLENWOOD BOY
Drum Solo

No. **4.** Flam
No. **6.** Flam Paradiddle
No. **7.** Flamacue
No. **2.** Five Stroke Roll

No. **3.** Seven Stroke Roll
No. **15.** Nine Stroke Roll
No. **20.** Flam Tap
No. **12.** Single Ratamacue

No. **13.** Triple Ratamacue
No. **26.** Double Ratamacue
No. **23.** Drag Paradiddle No. 2
No. **25.** Lesson 25

HARR

THE FIRST THIRTEEN
Drum Solo

THE SECOND THIRTEEN
Drum Solo

Featuring the second thirteen rudiments:

No. **14.** Single Stroke Roll   No. **18.** Thirteen Stroke Roll   No. **23.** Drag Paradiddle No. 2
No. **15.** Nine Stroke Roll   No. **19.** Fifteen Stroke Roll   No. **24.** Flam Paradiddle-diddle
No. **16.** Ten Stroke Roll   No. **20.** Flam Tap   No. **25.** Lesson 25
No. **17.** Eleven Stroke Roll   No. **21.** Single Paradiddle   No. **26.** Double Ratamacue
                                  No. **22.** Drag Paradiddle No. 1

HARR

BUNKER HILL

Rudiments used: Drum Solo

Flams	Double Paradiddle	Single Ratamacue	Drag Paradiddle No. 2
Flamacue	Compound Stroke No.1	7 Stroke Roll	Triple Ratamacue
Flam Paradiddle	Compound Stroke No. 2	Lesson 25	Flam Tap

HARR

THE DOWNFALL OF PARIS

(Eastern States version)

Drum Solo

This arrangement of THE DOWNFALL OF PARIS has the sticking used in the eastern states. The variation of sticking is in the first measure, the first three notes and the grace note are played with the right hand, the next three notes and the following grace note are played with the left hand. In the arrangement on the previous page, the first measure is sticked the same as the flam accent. I would advise the student to familiarize himself with both systems, then when playing in a contest, have the judge declare himself as to which method of sticking he prefers.

COLONEL IRONS

Drum Ensemble

For three Snare Drums, Cymbals and Bass Drum

C. R. HACKNEY
H. W. HARR

Colonel Irons (continued)

Colonel Irons (continued)